I'm Loving My Age

I'm Loving My Age

A Believer's Guide to Aging Gracefully and Words of Hope for the Elderly

by

Andrea Clarke Pratt

Xulon Press

Xulon Press
2301 Lucien Way #415
Maitland, FL 32751
407.339.4217
www.xulonpress.com

Printed in the United States of America.

ISBN-13: 978-1-6322-1582-6

Table of Contents

Dedication

I dedicate this book to three women who have been my significant sources of strength and inspiration: my mother, Reverend Yvonne Clarke, and my two deceased grandmothers, Mrs. Emma Pinder and Mrs. Georgianna Clarke.

"Favour is deceitful, and beauty is vain: but a woman that feareth the Lord, she shall be praised".

Proverbs 31:30

Book Acknowledgment

I would be remiss if I did not acknowledge the people who have been a source of inspiration in my life over the years.

I am thankful for the support of my leaders, Bishop Dr. Trevor Williamson and Pastor Sharon Williamson of the Trinity Global Cathedral.

I wish to also recognize Bishop Dr. Carrington S. Pinder, Reverend Dr. Sabrina Pinder, Reverend Dr. Sandra Knowles, Mrs. Brianna Bannister, and Mrs. Audrey Dean Rolle.

Last, but certainly not least, I thank my husband, Pastor Edward Pratt, and my family.

Introduction

"Grow old along with me!
The best is yet to be.
The last of life, for which the first was made."

– Robert Browning,
"Rabbi Ben Ezra"

This poem was one of my favorites as a teen, and now, so many years later, I still agree with the words penned by the great poet Robert Browning in his masterpiece, "Rabbi Ben Ezra"—**the best is yet to be.**

Doesn't it annoy you when you reach a certain age and people just want you to move out of the way and treat you like a building 'scaffold' that is no longer useful? You are expected to just sit back and watch life pass you by. I have been there and it is not a good feeling. Well, it is time to take back your life.

By investing just a few minutes a day with me meditating on God's word, you will learn biblical treasures for dealing with issues involving aging. Your life is not over; enjoy your present and know with surety that your best days are yet to come.

Each chapter of this book was inspired because of issues I, a family member, or a close friend experienced. For example, the topic *"El Roi, The God Who Sees Me: Resisting Loneliness and Recovering from Loss"* was birthed from my experience with the painful agony of death, having lost my grandmothers, father and only sister to it. *"Give Me My Mountain: Obtaining the Promises of God Despite Limitations"* was written to share with others the biblical principles which have helped me to overcome limitations that the world tried to place upon me.

The prayers at the end of each chapter may seem simple but are explosive. I believe the Holy Spirit guided me as I wrote each prayer using the Word of God and that there is power in them to destroy yokes and break chains. Pay special attention to praying them as you complete each chapter.

When looking into the eyes of many of the elderly in today's society, I have seen the pain in far too many individuals who have contributed so much to society but are now rejected by that same society. Many have voiced their pain and loneliness to me and I felt compelled by God to write this book.

As you age, you are simply a beautiful rose that is still opening. There is much wisdom in you that is waiting to be explored. The lives of the elderly should not be viewed as disposable. Aging is not something to be ashamed of as the western cultures make it seem. On the contrary, it is something to embrace and be thankful for, it is a gift from God. Many people did not survive the difficulties you had to endure but succumbed to addictions, or their difficulties could have led to their death. Yet you are still here; to God be the Glory!

Is it even possible to define the term *old age*? The World Health Organization (WHO) has observed that many developed countries regard 65 to be the definition of 'elderly' or older persons and the ages sixty to sixty-five as the onset of old age. However, it also noted that there is no typical person we can classify as elderly, as there are cases where some people who are eighty years of age have the physical and mental abilities of people who are only twenty years of age. I believe we all know at least one person like this.

Does the Bible define old age? According to *Strong's Concordance*, the Greek word for old age is *gèras*. This word was used when the angel Gabriel revealed to the Virgin Mary during Annunciation that her cousin Elizabeth, "is going to have a child in her old age" (Luke 1:36). Yes, Elizabeth was considered old, but there was a great blessing in store for her.

In the Old Testament, according to *Strong's Concordance*, the Hebrew word *Zaqen* is used to refer to the old; for instance, in Genesis 24:1, Abraham is referred to as *very old* or advanced in age. Abraham may have been considered *very old* but he had a faith in God that was explosive.

Strong's Concordance also notes that in some cases, *elder* may refer to someone having authority because of experience. According to Baker's Reference Library's *Evangelical Dictionary of Biblical Theology*, the term *yases* was used to refer to older persons who were helpless, as mentioned in 2 Chronicles 36:17, and the term *yaso* referred to persons worthy of respect due to their age.

Perhaps we may not live to be as old as the oldest person did in the Bible, but we can live a truly rewarding life. The longest living person in the Bible was Methuselah who died at the ripe, old age of 969. Although humans do not live as long as that nowadays, they are living longer than the people who lived a few centuries ago, possibly because of improved healthcare. With God's help, we can make every day we are on earth meaningful.

Life is not over for you. As soon as you start applying the principles in this book to your life, know that God's Holy Spirit will strengthen you to overcome any challenges you may face in the present, and better days will come.

How often in life do we long for the future or the past instead of embracing the blessings the present has to offer? When we were twelve years old, we longed for the day we would turn sixteen years of age; and when we become what some would call a *senior citizen* or *precious pearl*, we long for the good old days. When we are single, we long for married life, but when we are married, we remember the days we could be carefree and single. Let us endeavor to make the most of each moment and season in our life while having a vision and hope for a glorious future.

This book was not intended as a substitute for the medical advice physicians give but simply to remind you of the fact that you are of value to God and there is yet a purpose for your life. It was written to remind you that regardless of your age, God says, "For I know the plans I have for you," declares the Lord, "plans to prosper you and not to harm you, plans to give you hope and a future" (Jer. 29:11 NIV). You are an atom of potential, and with the help of God you will thrive even in the worst situation.

The treasures I found in the greatest book ever written, the Bible, helped my family and I, and I am sure they will help you. There is not a better time to get started than now. As you read this book, I pray you enjoy this journey and boldly declare with me, "I'm loving my age!"

Chapter One

Get Ready to Conquer the World: Dealing with Societal Ignorance

"I feel so useless!" Sybil proclaimed, as she sat idly at home. It had been years since her retirement, following forty years of work at the same company. Her husband, Harry, had passed away five years ago and her children and grandchildren, whom she had spent so many years doting upon, had all grown, now having families and interests of their own. She sometimes felt like a nuisance when she telephoned them. Sybil had returned from the mall an hour earlier, but while there, she had felt like an alien, ancient indeed, among so many youth. She often felt the disdain of the people who were annoyed at the slowness of her steps in the fast-paced environment.

Feeling Loved in a Narcissistic Society

What do you do when society no longer seems to want or need you? In many societies that exist today, the honor that was previously given to people as they *matured* in life has been replaced with irritation, rejection, disdain, and, in some cases, hostility or abuse. However, there are some cultures, such as Korean and Indian cultures, where much respect is still given to the elderly and aging is not looked down upon as something to be ashamed of but, rather, is celebrated. Sadly, it is often in the western cultures where the aged are marginalized. Ageism is a term that was first coined by Robert Neil Butler in 1969; it predominantly speaks about the discrimination against the aged. We see far too much of this today. However, do not allow the society you live in to diminish the value God has placed on your life.

Apostle Paul wrote the following concerning the time we are living in, *"For people will love only themselves and their money. They will be boastful and proud, scoffing at God, disobedient to their parents, and ungrateful. They will consider nothing sacred"* (2 Tim. 3:2 NLT). Indeed, we have become a very narcissistic society. In such a time as this when the aged often feel invisible or apologetic for still being alive, this book was written to encourage the not so young and simply say that God still remembers you. He still knows the number of hairs on your head, you are significant and of value.

The pursuit of money, fame, and power has often led many to trivialize the importance of maintaining a significant and caring relationship with the patriarchs and matriarchs in the family. However, do not let this discourage you. The great love of God allows you to feel loved even in a narcissistic society. Greatness abides within you. Remember that, *"Greater is he that is in you, than he that is in the world"* (1 John 4:4). You are well able to overcome the ignorance regarding the elderly that is prevalent in today's society. There is still much for you to do regardless of whether your residence is a nursing home or a condo.

There are many ways you can overcome feelings of uselessness or alienation from society and instead, utilize your golden years effectively and conquer societal ignorance God's way.

Avoid Becoming A Recluse

Do not live the life of a recluse in your latter years. Conquer the urge to allow societal ignorance to paralyze your spirit with fear and cause you to withdraw from society.

Continue to fellowship with others. I have some fantastic people I fellowship with at my local church and also some very dear family members and friends who have been there for me through good and bad times: Karen Dorsett, Kayla Dean, Patricia Johnson, Delores Fisher and Anna Skeete. All believers should fellowship with other believers, regardless of differences in age. As you interact with other believers, your faith can be strengthened, and you will build support. In the book of Ecclesiastes 4:9–10, we read, "Two are better than one; because they have a good reward for their labor. For if they fall, the one will lift up his fellow: but woe to him that is alone when he falleth; for he hath not another to help him up."

Even if you are not a believer in Jesus Christ, find someone to partner with. I have found in life, as you may have also, that the number of people you call your friends is not as important as the number of people who are faithful and true to you. At this point in my life, I prefer a few loyal friends than a network of disloyal frenemies.

Pray, Pray, Pray

Instead of focusing on societies' ignorance of the value of the aged, utilize your golden years to pray ever more fervently for your loved ones and particularly, for your children and descendants. Ask God to break any generational curses, destroy any evil altars, and release blessings upon your children.

God may have given you a vision of something He wants you to complete. Pray for God's grace to complete His assignment for your life and do not allow age discrimination in your society and the world to stop you from fulfilling that assignment. You are a kingdom citizen (a citizen of the kingdom of God) and one thing God has given to you is dominion, not over people, but rather over your sphere of influence.

The Glass Cell

Merriam-Webster dictionary defines the term *glass ceiling* as an, "intangible barrier within a hierarchy that prevents women or minorities from obtaining upper-level positions." Many elderly face something similar to the glass ceiling which I would term the *glass cell*. Many people in society believe that the elderly have nothing left to offer and should just move out of the way, sit in a rocking chair and watch life pass them by. I am here to tell you it is time for you to break out of that glass prison cell, dominate, and become all that God has called you to be.

Kingdom Mentorship

It is also time to conquer societal ignorance by demonstrating your value through training the next generation. Set a fine example and use your past mistakes to offer godly counsel. In his Epistle to Titus, The Apostle Paul provides a perfect example of this when he states,

Older men are to be sober-minded, dignified, self-controlled, sound in faith, in love, and in steadfastness. Older women likewise are to be reverent in behavior, not slanders or slaves to much wine (Titus 2:2–3 ESV).

Endeavor to motivate the youth to maximize their God-given potential. Impart to them some of the wisdom you have gained over the years.

Believe me when I say that young people often need godly counsel in the areas of finance, relationships, and work-life balance. I had a boss, while I was in my twenties, whose financial advice still has a positive impact on me even today.

Experiences you may have encountered in your life may have brought you to the brink of hell, but you can use those experiences as a testimony to others. Your God-given gifts can be imparted to others. My grandmother Emma was a great poetry lover and her enthusiasm was a catalyst for my love of reading and writing. She was able to set a fine example that impacted another generation. You can too.

How Does God View The Aged?

God's view of the aged and the way older people should be treated in society is made clear in the Bible. We can see an example of this in Leviticus 19:32, when He instructs people to rise in their presence and give them honor. Again, we see His view in Proverbs 16:31, "The hoary head is a crown of glory, if it be found in the way of righteousness," and in Proverbs 20:29, "The glory of young men is their strength: and the beauty of old men is the grey head."

This does not mean that all older people are wiser than those still in their youth; there is a wisdom that only obedience to God can bring. King David in Psalms 119:100 taught how he understood even more than persons who were older than him because he obeyed the commands of God and God revealed truth to him. Yes, many young people do have godly wisdom; however, it cannot be ignored that many things are learned only as we age, as stated in Job 12:12, "With the ancient is wisdom; and in length of days understanding."

Conquering the World

So, are you ready to conquer the world? Conquering the world may mean becoming an activist against ageism and some of you may have been anointed by

God to do just that. However, I am not referring to that. I am referring to simpler aspects like maintaining contact with the outside world to avoid becoming a recluse. I am referring to maintaining hope and a vision, for, "where there is no vision, the people perish" (Prov. 29:18). I am referring to conquering the world by not allowing the world to box you in and limit you.

Regardless of society's views on aging and any unkind words or actions displayed by them, do not allow any negative feelings to creep into your spirit. Rather, remember that God sees beauty in all ages, and whatever the obstacles, you are well able to defeat them. Make a decision today to conquer societal ignorance in God's way.

Daily To-Do List and Action Plan

1. Interact with society daily even if it is through the telephone to avoid becoming a recluse.
2. Pray daily for your children and descendants.
3. Become a mentor to someone.
4. Break out of the boundaries of the glass cell; say "No" to limitations, discriminations and prejudices.

Prayer

Heavenly Father,

I give you thanks and praise for your many blessings over the years. Father, I refuse to allow society's ignorance regarding the elderly to discourage me or consume me with bitterness. Your Son came to set the captives free! Let every yoke that societal ignorance has placed upon me be broken with your rod of iron and dashed into pieces like a potter's vessel. I believe only your report concerning me; you are aware of even the number of hairs on my head and you still have a plan and a purpose for my life. I rest in your words and I pray that you touch the hardened hearts in society.

In Jesus Christ's name.

Chapter Two

Do Not Call Me Mara: Battling Disappointment and Bitterness

$\mathcal{H}$ow many of us know that life presents us with many hurdles and disappointments along the way? Spouses leave, money invested in children seems almost fruitless, and loyalty and faithfulness toward your job go unrewarded. Do not allow these disappointments to make you bitter.

Is This Naomi?

The Bible speaks of Naomi who left Bethlehem-Judah due to a famine. She, along with her husband, Elimelech, and their two sons, moved to Moab. But while there, her husband died. Her sons grew and later married, but about ten years later, her two sons also died. As many have said, we expect our children to bury us, we do not expect to bury them. Upon learning that there was no longer a famine in Bethlehem, Naomi decided to return. She advised her daughters-in-law, Ruth and Orpah, to return to the homes of their mothers. Orpah decides to return to her mother, but Ruth clings to Naomi and insists on joining her mother-in-law as she returned to Bethlehem.

As they reach Bethlehem, long lost family and friends run out to greet them. They can barely believe it is Naomi who has come home. They ask, "Is this Naomi?" Perhaps she looked different due to the pain she had to endure over the years. Sometimes, life will do that to you. She replied to her people, "Call me not Naomi, call me Mara, for the Almighty hath dealt very bitterly with me. I went out full, and the Lord has brought me home empty; why then call ye me Naomi, seeing the Lord hath testified against me, and the Almighty hath afflicted me?" (Ruth 1:20-21). In Hebrew, Naomi's name meant pleasant or sweet but Mara meant bitter.

Naomi was bitter. Do not allow bitterness or disappointment to spoil your golden years and, most certainly, do not call yourself 'Mara.' God was not finished with her yet, destiny was calling. Ruth catches the fancy of a wealthy distant relative of Naomi named Boaz who had heard about the kindness Ruth had extended to her mother-in-law. Ruth wondered why he was so kind to her, but he mentioned to her how people had reported to him the compassion she had displayed toward her mother-in-law since the death of her husband. He even mentioned to Ruth how people related to him the enormous sacrifice and devotion she displayed by leaving her mother and father to travel to a strange land to accompany her mother-in-law. I believe if people fully comprehend the blessings that are bestowed from God as a result of caring for the elderly, more people would rush to their rescue.

Boaz and Ruth married and they had a child named Obed who was the father of Jesse, the father of King David. Women in Bethlehem later praised God for how he restored Naomi's life and sustained her in old age using a daughter-in-law who loved her so much, and was better to her than if she had given birth to seven sons.

The Bible states that Naomi became a nurse for the child. The Lord turned the circumstances around in Naomi's life. Her mourning was turned into joy. The heaviness in her heart was turned into praise. He can do the same for you. God has a way of giving you, "beauty for ashes, the oil of joy for mourning, the garment of praise for the spirit of heaviness" (Isa.

61:3). I have seen God turn around so many painful circumstances in my life where it could have been so easy to become bitter, but after I placed my trust in God, I watched Him turn the situation around into something good. God can truly turn a disappointing or hopeless season into a season of tremendous blessing.

Believe That Better Days Are Coming

No matter what arrow the enemy has hurled to destroy your life, declare as Joseph did after God raised him up although he had been rejected by his brothers and sold by them into slavery, "But as for you, ye thought evil against me; but God meant it unto good, to bring to pass, as it is this day, to save much people alive" (Gen. 50:20 NKJV). In fact, "No weapon that is formed against you shall prosper!" (Isa. 54:17). God is well able to turn what was meant to harm you into a blessing.

There are times when even one's children may be the cause of disappointment or pain as mentioned in Proverbs 17:25, "A foolish son is a grief to his father, and a bitterness to her that bare him." However, bitterness is the cause of many illnesses. Do not let their actions destroy you.

Chronic Complainers May Not Receive the Promise

Bitterness or disappointment can also lead many people to complain about everything. This displeases God. After He had delivered the children of Israel from 400 years of slavery in Egypt, many of the Israelites who had witnessed God's signs and wonders in bringing about their deliverance constantly complained about everything in the wilderness. Despite seeing the miracles, signs, and wonders God had performed before their very eyes, they complained; their constant complaints then reached a breaking point as stated in Numbers 14:11–12, "And the Lord said unto Moses, 'How long will this people provoke me? And how long will it be ere they believe me, for all the signs which I have shewed among them? I will smite them with the pestilence, and disinherit them, and will make of thee a greater nation and mightier than they.'" As a result of their constant complaining, God allowed only Caleb and Joshua to enter the Promised Land. Not one of those chronic complainers entered the land of Canaan.

Do you agree with me that in today's society, complaining on radio shows has seemed to become a national pastime? Do not become a chronic complainer; replace the complaints with thankfulness to God for His blessings. I am positive we can all find something to give God thanks for even if it's only for the breath we breathe. God will supply the strength you need to overcome bitterness. Allow Him to strengthen and restore you as you continue to remain content in Him, prepared for His use, and He has promised, "With long life, I will satisfy him and shew him my salvation" (Ps. 91:16).

Forgiveness is a Key to Your Victory

The Senior Pastor at my place of worship, Bishop Trevor Williamson, often speaks of the importance of forgiveness. Bitterness can stem from having an unforgiving heart. Unforgiveness is similar to having a beautiful mansion that is being eaten away by termites. The mansion is slowly crumbling, not because it was demolished from the outside, but from within. We must not allow anything or anyone to hinder our entrance into heaven. Many victories have not been achieved because people could not bring themselves to forgive others and therefore missed out on a greater blessing.

What Is Your Name?

No, your name is certainly not Mara. Perhaps your name is author, perhaps general in God's army, perhaps encourager, but it certainly is not Mara. Do not allow bitterness and disappointment to hinder your ability to fulfill God's purpose for your life. Celebrity newscaster, John Cameron Swayze, said about the Timex watch in the famous advertisement, "It takes a licking and keeps on ticking." Continue to press on. Though you may have had to take many *lickings* over the years, keep on *ticking*. God is not finished with you yet. Your life still has another chapter, a chapter that ends in victory.

Daily To-Do List and Action Plan

1. Read Isaiah 61:1-3, Psalms 73:21-26, and Psalms 23.
2. Find at least three things every day which you can give God thanks for.
3. Each day, reject the spirit of bitterness.
4. Proclaim boldly that all things are working together for your good.

Prayer

Heavenly Father,

I will bless you at all times! Your praises will continually be in my mouth. Father, I will not allow losses or the pain of the past to draw me into sorrow. I understand that you are constantly working everything out for my good. I ask you to remove this spirit of heaviness inside me and replace it by draping me in a garment of joy. Send out your fiery arrows and scatter the evil devices the enemy targeted against me. Thank you for allowing me to see so many years. I still know that you are able to do exceedingly and abundantly above all I can ask for or imagine according to the power that works in me!

In Jesus Christ's name.

Chapter Three

Give Me My Mountain: Obtaining the Promises of God Despite Limitations

*H*as God made you a promise you have not yet received? Were you expecting something, but it has not yet come to pass? Do not relinquish your dreams regardless of how much you have advanced in years. When I think of an individual who refused to let his age prevent him from obtaining His promise from God, I think of Caleb and his tenacity.

Focusing on the Promise and Not On the Problem

Moses had sent Joshua and Caleb along with ten other spies into the land of Canaan to spy on the land before entering it with the children of Israel. When the twelve spies returned, they declared that the land was indeed a fruitful land. Caleb excitedly stated, "Let us go up at once, and possess it; for we are well able to overcome it" (Num. 13:30).

But all of the other spies, except for Joshua, said they could not do that, "And we even saw giants there, the descendants of Anak. We felt as small as grasshoppers, and that is how we must have looked to them" (Num. 13:33 GNT). Do you see yourself as a grasshopper in comparison to the obstacle which is hindering you from obtaining the promise of God? Stop focusing on your strength and your power and how formidable your obstacle is; instead, focus on the power and greatness of the God you serve. He is omnipotent.

Many years later, when Caleb was eighty-five years old, we see his courage again. He focused not on his limitations but on the limitless God he served. In Joshua 14:10–12, Caleb declares:

[10] And now, behold, the Lord hath kept me alive, as he said, these forty and five years, even since the Lord spake this word unto Moses, while the children of Israel wandered in the wilderness: and now, lo, I am this day fourscore and five years old.

[11] As yet I am as strong this day as I was in the day that Moses sent me: as my strength was then, even

so is my strength now, for war, both to go out, and to come in.

¹² Now therefore give me this mountain, whereof the Lord spake in that day; for thou heardest in that day how the Anakims were there, and that the cities were great and fenced: if so be the Lord will be with me, then I shall be able to drive them out, as the Lord said.

This is an eighty-five-year-old man declaring that he is as strong now as he was forty years ago. And he's telling Joshua that the Lord had promised him the land years ago; and now he wants his land, the one with the giants, whom he will then drive out. He boldly declares, "Give me my mountain!" God had made a promise to Caleb years before, and he was determined to obtain that promise. What has God promised you? God is not finished with you yet.

The Power of Using Faith Filled Words to Obtain the Promises of God

Caleb and Joshua's words were so positive and not brimmed with the negativity of the other spies. Are your words faith-filled or fear-filled? What type of words do you speak concerning yourself and your abilities? We must be mindful of the benefits of self-affirmation and the power of spoken words. The Bible states, "Death and life are in the power of the tongue,

And those who love it will eat its fruit" (Prov. 18:21). It also states, "The words that I speak unto you, they are spirit, and they are life" (John 6:63). Too many people believe it is a sign of humility to speak words belittling themselves.

One of the most powerful books I have ever read was written by Dr. Leroy Thompson, Sr., "How to Speak the Word of God with the Voice of Jesus." In his book, Dr. Thompson speaks of the importance of not simply confessing the Word of God, but rather meditating on the Word of God until the very words you have meditated on become real to you (or a Rhema word) and produce manifestation.

Consistently meditate on scriptures concerning you until those words become alive in your spirit. As an author, my meditations are on the scriptures Jeremiah 30:2, Matthew 13:51-52, Psalms 45:1, and Revelations 21:5. Meditate on God's Word, then proclaim those life-filled words, and watch long lost dreams become realities.

Wrestling To Obtain Your Promise

How badly do you want the *mountain* God has promised you? Do you have the faith of Jacob to wrestle until your situation changes? In Genesis 32:24, we read the story of how Jacob wrestled with a man until daybreak. At the break of day, the man entreated

Jacob to let him go but Jacob boldly proclaimed, "I will not let you go until you bless me." After the wrestling match, the man told Jacob, *"Your name will no longer be Jacob, but Israel, because you have struggled with God and with humans and have overcome"* (Gen. 32:28 NIV). What are you struggling with? Jacob is said to have a bulldog kind of faith that refuses to let go. Is your faith like Jacob's or do you run away at the first sign of a struggle? Grab ahold of God's promises in His Word, utilize the weapon of prayer, and do not let go until you obtain the prize.

Too Old According to Man, But the Perfect Age for God

Isn't it amazing how we can see, all through the Scripture, God using people who men would have rejected or who they may have thought unworthy? There are no limitations in His eyes, and He sees value in each individual. All He needs is a willing and obedient vessel. The same is true with age. At the age of seventy-five, God told Abram (who was later renamed Abraham by God) to leave his country and his family and travel to a land unknown by him and that He would bless him substantially, even blessing those who blessed him.

He did not ask Abram to do this at the age of twenty-five when he was strong and virile. He did not even tell him this at thirty-five. No, He waited until Abram was seventy-five to call him. God had a significant purpose for Abram at the age of seventy-five; so, regardless of your age, God has a purpose and a plan for your life as well. He is not finished with you yet. Your latter shall be greater than your former. God gave Abram a word and this man of faith unquestioningly acted upon that word. Obediently, he left his home as God had instructed.

The lives of Abraham and his wife, Sarah, were filled with testimonies that age does not limit God and that nothing is too hard for Him. In addition to being called by God to do this great work at the age of seventy-five, it was at the age of ninety that God told Abraham that his wife Sarah would bear him a son the following year. She gave birth when she was ninety-one years old. In Genesis 18:14, God tells Abraham, "Is anything too hard for the Lord?"

God Himself is not bound by human limitations. He often chooses people to perform an assignment when things seem impossible as a result of circumstances and human frailties. The Bible does not even mention the word retirement. Although old people may have been physically incapable of officially performing certain roles, they went on to instruct the younger generation.

To obtain that promise of God or complete the vision God has given to you, it is important that you be mindful of the scripture that states:

So be careful how you live. Don't live like fools, but like those who are wise. Make the most of every opportunity in these evil days. Don't act thoughtlessly, but understand what the Lord wants you to do (Eph. 5:15–18 NLT).

You need to redeem the time, or as the Bible states in the scripture I mentioned earlier, "make the most of every opportunity."

Give Me My Mountain

Don't let the devil steal anything from you in this season. Don't let your age or anything stop you from going after your dream, but continue to declare as Caleb did, "Give me this mountain" (Josh. 14:12). Continue to stand on the promises God has given you and which were declared in His Word. Those promises may be the salvation of your loved ones, a new business, or mortgage cancellation; whatever it is, continue to stand. God is the Alpha and Omega, the beginning and the end. Do not give up on the dream God has given you. Step out on faith. I repeat, step out on faith. Pick up your Bible from wherever you left it and continue to stand on God's promises. Some of these promises may be experienced by your descendants, and others will be received by you personally, "For all the promises of God in Him are Yes, and in Him Amen, to the glory of God through us" (2 Cor. 1:20 NKJV).

Daily To-Do List and Action Plan

1. Read Psalms 1 and Joshua 1:1-18.
2. Write down the vision and dreams God has placed in your heart.
3. Meditate and pray the scriptures that confirm those visions and dreams.
4. Speak positive affirmations about yourself and meditate daily on the Word of God until it becomes a rhema in your spirit.
5. Decide today that you will not give up on the promises God has made to you.

Prayer

Heavenly Father,

You are an awesome God and there is none like you! I stand firmly on your promises to me and will not look to the right or the left. You are Alpha and Omega, the beginning and the end, and I know that you are well able to complete what you have started in my life. I will step out on faith trusting in your Word, and I know that I can do all things through Christ that strengthens me. Let your mercy surround me. I refuse to look at my limitations because I know that greater is He that is in me than he that is in the world. Thank you, Father, because I believe that you will make my latter greater than my former!

In Jesus Christ's name.

Chapter Four

Not Guilty: Rebounding from Regrets

"I hate you! All you caused our family was pain!" Angelique shouted at her dad and left, slamming the door behind her. John lived alone and wept bitterly because he knew she had all the right to feel the way she did. He had been an alcoholic for many years and had verbally and physically abused his family before his wife finally decided they had enough and left with their children. As an old man now, he had come to realize his faults, and the hopelessness of reconciliation weighed heavily upon his frail shoulders.

There are many people who, like John, feel deep regret over their past actions. Quite often, we are plagued with regrets as we age. Most of life's regrets can be placed in two categories: those which are not sinful in nature, and those that are.

Regretting Life Choices

Sometimes regrets stem from decisions we made, which, although not sinful, we later realize were not the best choice for us. For example, many people regret not spending more time with their families. They regret not doing a better job of balancing their work and personal lives as they had invested most of their time in building their careers at the expense of their family lives because of which their children and other members of their family are now like strangers to them. On the other hand, many people may have sacrificed their careers to devote their time to their families and in the process, felt like they lost their self-identity and that they did not maximize their true potential. Others regret not having children, the relationship choices they made, or other decisions taken over the years. If you are dealing with regrets such as these, you can hold fast to the promises of God and rise above the emotions that are weighing you down.

The apostle Peter was able to overcome the deep regret he felt after denying Jesus three times. When all of the disciples had gathered together with Jesus to celebrate the Jewish celebration of the Feast of Passover, Jesus told his disciples, "All ye shall be offended because of me this night: for it is written, I will smite the shepherd and the sheep of the flock will scattered abroad" (Matt. 26:31). But Peter, bold as usual, told Jesus that he would never deny him. Jesus then told Peter, "Verily I say unto thee, that this day, even in this night, before the cock crow twice, thou shall deny me thrice" (Mark. 14:30). How did Peter respond to Jesus after being told this? Peter, again self-confident as usual, vehemently proclaimed to Jesus, "If I should die with thee, I will not deny thee in any wise" (Mark. 14:31). After Peter declared this, all the disciples joined in and proclaimed their loyalty to Jesus. Later that night, as Jesus had prophesied, Peter denied having known Jesus on three occasions. He swore that he did not know Him, "Then began he to curse and to swear, saying, 'I know not the man.' And immediately the cock crew. And Peter remembered the word of Jesus, which said unto him, Before the cock crow, thou shalt deny me thrice. And he went out, and wept bitterly" (Matt. 26: 74–75).

Peter deeply regretted denying Jesus, but later, with God's help, he overcame this regret, his life was transformed, and he was converted to a general in the faith. It is time for you to move from living in the land of regret.

The apostle Paul puts it this way when he writes to the Philippians:

Brethren, I count not myself to have apprehended: but this one thing I do, forgetting those things which are behind, and reaching forth unto those things which are before, I press toward the mark for the prize of the high calling of God in Christ Jesus (Phil. 3: 13–14).

Paul likens our Christian journey to running a race; if we glance behind us as we are running, it will only serve to slow us down.

I am sure Paul, who before his conversion was called Saul, later regretted his role in the death of the first Christian martyr, Stephen. It is described in Acts 7:58, "And cast him out of the city, and stoned him: and the witnesses laid down their clothes at a young man's feet, whose name was Saul." And later, we read the verses, "Saul approved of putting Stephen to death" (Acts 8:1 GW). However, Paul refused to live a life wallowing in self-pity and was determined to *press toward the mark*.

Ask God to turn all those regrets into opportunities for His glory to be revealed. Believe me, He has resurrection power even in the worst situations. Brothers and sisters, it is time to bury those regrets and to press on in the Lord.

Regretting Sinful Actions

Sometimes, regrets may stem from decisions that we made that were sinful in nature. Illicit affairs, verbal or physical abuse of family or friends, theft, or murder may lead to much regret. However, if you are suffering from regret or even shame or guilt because of something that you did which was sinful in nature, there is a major question you must ask yourself, are you simply filled with regret or are you also repentant?

About those who are genuinely remorseful for the sins they have committed, the Bible declares in Matthew 5:4, "Blessed are they that mourn: for they shall be comforted." Some mourn over the sins they committed, similar to someone who is mourning the death of a loved one. They not only regret what they have done but now also hate sin and the distance it creates between themselves and God and desire to be free from it. True repentance bears some fruits. John the Baptist proclaimed this when he told the Pharisees, "Bring forth therefore fruits meet for repentance" (Matt. 3:8). We can understand it better if we read a translation of God's Word, "Do those things that prove you have turned to God and have changed the way you think and act" (Luke 3:8 GW).

To those of us who are truly repentant for our sins, God mercifully states, "If we confess our sins, he is faithful and just to forgive us our sins, and to cleanse us from all unrighteousness" (1 John 1:9). No matter what the sin or how filthy you may feel because of it, the powerful blood of Jesus Christ can sanctify you and help you overcome the feelings of guilt, shame, and regret. Jesus can truly comfort you. It is one of the reasons He came, as stated in Isaiah 61: 1–2:

The Spirit of the Lord God is upon me; because the Lord hath anointed me to preach good tidings unto the meek; He hath sent me to bind up the brokenhearted, to proclaim liberty to the captives, and the opening of the prison to them that are bound; To proclaim the acceptable year of the Lord, and the day of vengeance of our God; to comfort all that mourn.

We have been declared *not guilty*. I believe I am guilty of breaking most of the Ten Commandments. However, upon giving my life to God, I can stand on the promise of Jesus that, "Though your sins are like scarlet, I will make them as white as snow" (Isa. 1:18 NLT). One of the statements Jesus declared on that rugged cross was, "It is finished" (John 19:30). The words are translated "Tetelestai" in Greek. To put these powerful words simply, Jesus was saying that with the shedding of His innocent blood, our sin debt was paid in full. We are no longer condemned. If we celebrate when someone pays off our financial debts for us, how much more should we celebrate with the sin debt Jesus paid on our behalf? Hallelujah!

There are people, however, who feel regret for prior sinful acts, but their regret is born simply out of guilt, fear, or dread of the consequences of their actions. Some people's regret may even stem from deep-rooted anger against God for allowing the situation to have occurred. These people do not manifest true repentance. Judas Iscariot is a prime example of this. After betraying Jesus, Judas Iscariot, the disciple of Jesus, felt much guilt for what he had done. This is described in Matthew 27:3 when Judas returned to the chief priests and elders the thirty pieces of silver they had given him to betray Jesus. Judas felt remorse for what he had done but was more overcome with guilt or dread of the consequences of his actions than being overwhelmed with a desire for reconciliation with God. He did not ask God for forgiveness but instead committed suicide.

If you are overcome with regrets or even shame or guilt because of something in your past or a decision you made, do not allow it to weigh you down. With Jesus's help, you are able to rebound from regrets and with the shedding of His blood, you no longer need to bear the guilt. You do not have to carry that burden; Christ already carried it for you.

As I go through situations in life that prove too much for me or the agony of guilt or regret try to weigh me down, I simply say to Jesus, "Lord I cast this situation on you, I need you to deal with it, I turn it over to you." He is able to turn a negative situation into something positive. He can bring hope to a hopeless situation. Rather than focusing on the regrets, give them to God and ask Him to show you how to use them as a stepping stone.

Daily To-Do List and Action Plan

1. Read Romans 10:9, Psalms 32:1-5, and Psalms 51:1-19 and repent of committing sins known and unknown.
2. Do not condemn yourself for past mistakes, but rest in knowing God loves you and you have been declared *not guilty*.

Prayer

Merciful Father,

I humbly come before You, asking You to look down with mercy upon me and wash me, cleanse me, and purge me. Wash away my iniquities, cleanse me from my sins, and purge me so that my scarlet sins are made as white as snow. Father, I repent for all my sins, known and unknown. Create in me a clean heart and renew a right spirit in me. Do not despise my broken heart. Allow me to see the goodness of the Lord once again in the land of the living. Mend the hearts of those to whom I have caused pain. Restore to me the years that the enemy has stolen for there is nothing too hard for you, and I will be mindful to give You all the praise, glory, and honor!

In Jesus Christ's name.

Chapter Five

I Left My Burdens Over There: Overcoming Anxiety and Worry

"Who will be there to take care of me when I can no longer take care of myself?" "Will my children ever receive my loving Savior into their lives?" "Is my pension enough to sustain me during my latter years?" Anxiety and worry consume the lives of people in different stages of their lives, and even to those who are more advanced in age, these psychological states are no exception.

Having enough funds to meet essential needs during retirement, failing health, the death of loved ones, and the fear of abandonment during a time of need are just some of the issues that may burden someone's heart.

The Spirit of Fear

At the heart or root of much of this anxiety and worry is fear. The spirit of fear can bring people to the point of mental confusion or even an early death if left unchecked. But God has not given you the spirit of fear; no, He has given you the spirit of power, love, and a sound mind (2 Tim. 1:7). First, He has given you power and strength in Him to overcome challenges. Second, He has given you a sound mind, not one void of self-control or paralyzed due to confusion. Lastly, He has given you a spirit of love and not bitterness or hate against the people who are treating you unjustly because of your age. Yes, you have the spirit of power, love, and a strong mind and dominion, in His name, over the spirit of fear. You have made it through many dangers, toils and snares, obstacles, and giants in the past; and you will make it through any future challenges to come.

Battling Anxiety and Worry With Thanksgiving

The apostle Paul spoke of anxiety in his Epistle to the Philippians when he wrote:

Be anxious for nothing, but in everything by prayer and supplication, with thanksgiving, let your requests be made known to God; and the peace of God, which surpasses all under-standing, will guard your hearts and minds through Christ Jesus" (Phil. 4:6).

Paul wrote this scripture at a time when many Bible scholars believe he was in prison, a circum-stance that can lead most into a state of anxiety or, at the very least, worry.

However, during this time, Paul offers clues as to how he was able to maintain peace under such a seemingly dismal situation. In the Scripture, he mentions the importance of prayer along with sup-plication and thanksgiving. Paul was showing that he was thankful in his situation. This is a very important weapon to use against anxiety and worry as it is very difficult to be thankful and anxious at the same time. Instead of worrying yourself into an early grave, pray and submit your needs before God. Giving thanks to God during the situation and giving it over to God helps in bringing peace to you.

The Friend Who Is Truly Able to Bare All of Your Burdens

A poem written by a gentleman named Joseph M. Scriven in 1855 to his sick mother was later turned into the well-known hymn, "What a Friend We Have in Jesus." I must include three verses of this hymn because they contain such meaning. Like so many other hymns, this one was written by someone who went through many sorrows and trials in his life but understood what a blessing it is to cast one's cares on the friend who is like none other and sticks closer than a brother, Jesus Christ (Prov. 18:24).

"What a friend we have in Jesus
All our sins and griefs to bear!
What a privilege to carry
Everything to God in prayer!
Oh what peace we often forfeit,
Oh what needless pain we bear,
All because we do not carry
Everything to God in prayer!

Have we trials and temptations?
Is there trouble anywhere?
We should never be discouraged,
Take it to the Lord in prayer.

Can we find a friend so faithful
Who will all our sorrows share?
Jesus knows our every weakness,
Take it to the Lord in prayer.

Are we weak and heavy-laden,
Cumbered with a load of care?

Precious Savior, still our refuge—
Take it to the Lord in prayer;
Do thy friends despise, forsake thee?
Take it to the Lord in prayer;
In His arms He'll take and shield thee,
Thou wilt find a solace there.

There is a popular saying that goes, "The arms of flesh will fail you, you dare not trust your own," which was taken from the hymn, "Stand Up, Stand Up for Jesus" (George Duffield, Jr. 1858). The Bible also states in Jeremiah 17:5, "Cursed be the man that trusteth in man, and maketh flesh his arm, and whose heart departeth from the Lord." As you get older, you will realize that even your closest friend can let you down at times and that though the arms of flesh will fail you, we have a true friend in Jesus. I can testify that He has never failed me and so He will not fail you either. As the song goes, take your burdens to the Lord in prayer instead of trying to bear them alone. Jesus states it plainly when he says:

Come unto me, all ye that labor and are heavy laden, and I will give you rest. Take my yoke upon you and learn of me; for I am meek and lowly in heart: and ye shall find rest unto your souls. For my yoke is easy, and my burden is light (Matt. 11:28–30).

Battling Fear with Faith In God

I love watching a sermon on YouTube entitled, "You Don't Have Any Trouble, All You Need is Faith in God," by the late, great American televangelist, R. W. Schambach.

In his typical fiery style, Shambach tells a story of a man who was on his death bed. Although the man was in a coma, he understood all that was going on around him. His priest gave him the last rites and after everyone left the hospital room, Doctor Jesus walked in.

Jesus told the man in the bed, "You, Don't have any Trouble, All you Need is Faith in God!" Jesus told the man He was healing him now and walked out of the room. The man lay in the bed pondering for a while over what had just been said to him and was bewildered considering he was on his death bed and had spent all his money on his sickness. But his faith increased and he got right up out of that bed, shaved and the nurse was shocked when she walked into the room and saw the empty bed then saw the man in the bathroom shaving and singing. Quench those blazing darts of worry and anxiety the devil is sending at you by picking up your shield; the shield of faith (Eph. 6:16). It only takes faith the size of a mustard seed for God to get things rolling in your life.

But there is one thing God will need you to do: trust in Him. Trust that He will never leave or forsake you. Trust that He has your back even if no one else does. Trust Him in times of prosperity, recession, and depression. Trust that He will turn situations around to work out for your good. Proverbs 3:5–6 declares, "Trust in the Lord with all your heart, and lean not on your own understanding. In all thy ways acknowledge Him, And He shall direct your paths." We have to trust God in all situations or we will not be pleasing in His eyes for, "Without faith it is impossible to please Him: for he who cometh to God must believe that He is, and that He is a rewarder of those who diligently seek Him" (Heb. 11:6).

Trusting God and having a thankful heart reduces the unfruitful time spent in your latter years as the result of being a chronic complainer. We do not want to be like the children of Israel who wandered in the wilderness for forty years when the journey should have only taken eleven days from Horeb by way of Mount Seir to Kadesh Barnea, as stated in Deuteronomy 1:2.

We are also admonished not to worry. The Scripture declares:

Are not five sparrows sold for two farthings, and not one of them is forgotten by God? But even the very hairs of your head are all numbered. Fear not therefore: ye are of more value than many sparrows (Luke 12:6-7).

God knows you by name; He knows where you are even right now, and therefore, it is useless to spend so much valuable time fretting in your latter years about things which may not even come to pass. You will not be made to feel ashamed and as King David stated, "I have been young and now am old; yet have I not seen the righteous forsaken nor his seed begging bread" (Ps. 37:25). Jesus tells us quite plainly in Matthew 6:25, not to worry about food, drink or clothing like those who do not believe in God, but rather He admonishes us in Matthew 6:33, "But seek ye first the kingdom of God, and his righteousness; and all these things shall be added unto you." The moral of the story is, stop worrying.

So, when you stop worrying, what will you be thinking about? The apostle Paul gives us an answer in Philippians 4:8:

Finally, brethren, whatsoever things are true, whatsoever things are honest, whatsoever things are just, whatsoever things are pure, whatsoever things are lovely, whatsoever things are of good report; if there be any virtue, and if there be any praise, think on these things.

God Is Your Sustainer; Let Go of the Burden

Always remember that God is your source. Sometimes we focus on our job and individuals when we have a need; however, God is our ultimate source. Talk to Him about your cares and your worries for He cares for you; do not give into the spirit of fear, but rather continue to be strong in Him for He has said, "Have I not commanded you? Be strong and of good courage; do not be afraid, nor be dismayed, for the Lord our God is with you wherever you go" (Josh. 1:9 NKJV).

So, have you left your burdens over there? "Where is over there?" you may ask. Over there is at the foot of the altar. Over there is with Jesus who has asked you to cast them upon Him. Do you have a suitcase of burdens loaded upon your back, or have you released the burdens and placed them over there?

Daily To-Do List and Action Plan

1. Read Psalms 23:1-6, Proverbs 3:5-6, and Psalms 20:1-9.
2. Thank God for all His blessings and let your requests be known to Him.
3. Visualize releasing yourself from your burdens and laying them before Jesus.
4. Be mindful not to meditate on your problems but rather meditate on God's promises.

Prayer

Heavenly Father,

I enter your courts with a spirit of thanksgiving! Thank you for your favor and your mercy upon my life and my family. You have not given me the spirit of fear but one of power, love, and a sound mind. Deliver my soul from the enemy and keep me alive in the time of famine. I refuse to let anxiety and worry dominate my thoughts; rather, I focus my mind on things that are noble, right, lovely, and praiseworthy. I cast all my cares upon you. I seek first only Your kingdom and Your way of doing things and I know, as a result, I will receive all that I need.

In Jesus Christ's name.

Chapter Six

El Roi, The God Who Sees Me: Resisting Loneliness and Recovering from Loss

"Everyone I love seems to be dying!" cried Emily. She was eighty-eight-years-old and had just returned home from her best friend Dianne's funeral. Over the last few years, she had lost many of her close friends and family to death. Sometimes, when something special happened in her life, she picked up the telephone to tell a family member or a friend only to put it down after remembering that person had passed.

Trust God Even in The Season of Loneliness

Aging often comes with a feeling of loneliness. Christmas and other special occasions are times when these feelings may be intensified as old people may become overwhelmed with feelings of loneliness. It is often during the Christmas holidays that people remember those who they lost through death. As you get older, the number of family and friends you've lost to death naturally increases. Memories of happier times may plague your heart. Disproportionate or imbalanced focus on negative aspects of your present situations may flood the mind and it could be quite easy to succumb to self-pity and the spirit of heaviness.

We read in an earlier chapter how Naomi felt at the loss of her husband and her two sons. Another biblical patriarch, Job, must have also felt a sense of loneliness when he cried out, "My voice is as sad and lonely as the cries of a jackal or an ostrich" (Job 30:29). He had lost so much; children, wealth, and health, and his wife and friends treated him with contempt and were not truly there for him when he needed them most. Suffering can truly result in a feeling of isolation. During this lonely time in Job's life, he maintained communication with God notwithstanding to lament. In the end, the Scripture shows that Job received double for this lonely time in his life. The

Word declares, "So the Lord blessed the latter end of Job more than his beginning..." (Job 42:12).

There are times in our lives when we will experience seasons of loneliness, pain, and suffering. However, better days will come as everything is but for a season. Ecclesiastes 3:1–2 puts it this way, "To everything there is a season, and a time to every purpose under the heaven: a time to be born, and a time to die; a time to plant, and a time to pluck up that which is planted." Trust God even during your season of loneliness and watch things turn in your favor.

How Long Will You Mourn?

There are times we may suffer a devastating loss or feel a sense of loneliness because of abandonment or rejection by others; perhaps due to a divorce, which may often feel like a death, or maybe neglect from the children for whom so many sacrifices were made. These can bring about a spirit of heaviness and the spirit of mourning of the loss of the valued relationship. Friends may go and friends may come. But the Bible says in Proverbs 18:24, "One who has unreliable friends soon comes to ruin, but there is a friend who sticks closer than a brother." Oh yes, friends may reject you, family members may turn their backs on you, there may be no prayer partner in sight, and you may have no one to run to, but Jesus is a friend like none other. King David declared, "When my father and my mother forsake me, then the Lord will take care of me." (Ps. 27:10 NKJV).

Yes, the loss of certain relationships can often result in a feeling of loneliness. But I am often reminded of the words of God as He spoke to Samuel who was emotionally consumed by his disappointment when God had rejected Saul after Saul had once again disobeyed God. God simply said to Samuel:

How long will you mourn for Saul seeing I have rejected him from reigning over Israel? Fill thine horn with oil, and go, I will send thee to Jesse, the Bethlehemite: For I have provided me a king among his sons" (1 Sam. 16:1 NKJV).

God was simply telling the prophet to stop wallowing in this situation, get up, and start focusing on the new assignment He had given him. Today. I am asking you this: How long will you keep your grave clothes on? For how much longer will you keep building your life based on the past? For how much longer will you immortalize something dead when God has something greater in store for you? It is time to tear those grave clothes off and pour yourself into releasing something into the lives of the living rather than focusing on what is dead. Do not get me wrong, the pain associated with the loss of a relationship is real. However, God kept you alive for a reason. God has something much better in store for you and a purpose and plan for your life. Therefore, arise, brush yourself off, wipe those tears, and start living again.

Sometimes, when an individual feels alone, they can feel like they are the only one going through a certain situation. Elijah felt like this after Jezebel threatened to kill him and he felt all alone. While he was on the run from her and had stopped to rest in a cave, he cried out to God, "...and I, even I only, am left; and they seek my life, to take it away." (1 Kings 19:10). Elijah thought that he was the only faithful servant of God who remained alive, but God told him, "Yet I have left me seven thousand in Israel, all the knees which have not bowed unto Baal, and every mouth which hath not kissed him" (1 Kings 19:18). You are not alone in what you are going through and God is aware of the location of each of his servants and the circumstances they are in.

Keys to Overcoming Loneliness

There are a few things you can do when you are feeling lonely to overcome at least some of its impact. Try to help someone else. Many times, when we forget about ourselves and circumstances for a moment and help others, it can rebuild our self-confidence and help us realize that others are in worse situations than us.

You can also make a list of the things you should thank God for, and I promise you, you will feel that loneliness begins to disappear.

Another way to lessen loneliness is to focus on a dormant gift you may have, whether it is cooking, sewing, or a particular sporting activity; try to move your focus away from the situation. Join clubs or church groups where you can meet others.

Do not forget that the Holy Spirit is our constant guide and companion. In my times of distress, I am often reminded of the Scripture verse in Isaiah 41:10, "Fear thou not for I am with thee: be not dismayed; for I am thy God. I will strengthen thee; yea, I will help thee; yea, I will uphold thee with the right hand of my righteousness."

God is with You

El–Roi is one of the names for God and is trans-lated, "the God who sees me." This name was intro-duced in Genesis 16:13 when Hagar, Sarai's Egyptian maid, fled into the wilderness away from her mistress. Hagar may have thought she was alone in that wil-derness, but God was right there with her. The angel of the Lord spoke to her in that lonely place and told her to return to her mistress and gave her a word about the son in her womb. Hagar responded by pro-claiming God to be a God who "sees me."

If you are lonely today or suffering from loss, know without a shadow of a doubt, God sees you. He is El Roi. He sees you and He cares. This too shall pass. You are never really alone.

Daily To-Do List and Action Plan

1. Read Romans 8:38–39.
2. Know that you are not alone in what you are going through.
3. Push through your pain and assist someone else.
4. Thank God for all His blessings.
5. Embrace and stir up your God-given gifts.

Prayer

Father, in the mighty name of Jesus, I worship and exalt You. I glorify Your name. I come casting my burdens upon You for they are too much for me to carry. I know that You are near me when I call. Father, I stand on Your Word that You will never leave nor forsake me and that the righteous will never be forsaken. You have promised to be with me even to the end of the ages. You have said that You are with me and that I have nothing to fear, for You will help me and uphold me with Your right hand. Thank You for binding up this broken heart of mine. Thank You for being a friend that sticks closer than a brother and for being a constant help even in times of trouble.

In Jesus Christ's name.

Chapter Seven

Get Ready for the Boomerang: Rewards for Blessing Seniors

We are going to sue this facility!" shouted Juanita at one of the supervisors at the nursing care facility where her mother resided. Juanita had prior suspicions that her mother was being abused and had planted a hidden camera in her mother's room. To her horror, the recording revealed her greatest fear.

The Example of Jesus

It is so sad that, like Juanita's mom, many seniors in today's society are verbally and physically abused. Many others are neglected. God's Word does not fail to provide instructions on how people in their golden years should be treated by others. One of the last words Jesus Himself said as He hung on the cross is to make provision for the care of His mother:

When Jesus, therefore, saw His mother, and the disciple whom He loved standing by, He said to His mother, "Woman, behold your son!" Then He said to the disciple, "Behold your mother!" And from that hour that disciple took her to his own home (John 19:26–27 NKJV).

If Jesus set such an example, shouldn't those who are also called Christians follow His example?

Admonitions from God

The Scripture is saturated with instructions and admonitions on how God expects parents and elders in society to be treated. Early in the scriptures, God stresses the importance of this when He included it in the Ten Commandments, "Honour thy father and thy mother: that thy days may be long upon the land which the Lord thy God giveth thee" (Exod. 20:12). We read something similar to this in Deuteronomy 5:16, but He also adds, "that it may go well for thee, in the land which the Lord thy God giveth thee." The New Testament further mentions honoring one's parents when Apostle Paul states, "Honour thy father and mother; which is the first commandment with promise; that it may be well with thee, and thou mayest live long on the earth." (Eph. 6:2–3). Once again, honoring one's parents is linked to the length of one's life and their circumstances in life.

Excuses and More Excuses

In today's world, with so many self-absorbed people, they find all sorts of excuses for not properly caring for parents. Other financial obligations seem to be much more important at the time than assisting parents who may be in need. There is so much to do at work or, perhaps, the children and husband require much time; sometimes, people become extremely busy at church or with some charitable or political organization. It may all seem for the greater good. However, sometimes, excuses that appear to be well-meaning on the surface are, in actuality, a skillful way of avoiding what is most important.

One day, the Pharisees questioned Jesus about why His disciples did not wash their hands before eating, which was a Jewish ritual. Jesus responded by telling them that they very skillfully avoided the commandment of God by following their own traditions. He gave the example of how they skillfully let people avoid following the commandment of honoring their father and mother by telling others:

But you say it is all right for people to say to their parents, "Sorry, I can't help you. For I have vowed to give to God what I would have given to you. In this way, you say they don't need to honor their parents. And so you cancel the word of God for the sake of your own tradition." You hypocrites! Isaiah was right when he prophesied about you, for he wrote "These people honor me with their lips, but their hearts are far from me. (Matt. 15:5–8 NLT).

They had deceitfully used their vow to God to disobey God's fifth commandment.

Things have not changed; children still find so many reasons to neglect parents and do not honor them. It is sad when we hear of cases where children have not even telephoned their parents for years. Yes, there are cases when the parents may have neglected or abused the child; however, I believe there is a special reward for a child who can forgive a parent and still honor that parent.

How Should the Elderly be Honored?

There are many ways we can honor someone. We can show reverence or respect toward a person through the things we say or do. Speaking to them respectfully rather than belittling them or being verbally abusive.

We can honor them by anticipating their needs even before they arise or having empathy to discern situations they may be facing. For example, a parent may feel embarrassed to say they are hungry and may not have money left for food. An empathetic, discerning child might know that the parent has such a need and either offer to buy food or provide money for their need. These are just a few examples.

Contrary to common belief, honor may involve more than showing respect; it may involve supplying tangible needs. There are blessings in store for those who, through a pure motive, provide you with food or shelter, speak kind words, or anticipate your needs. Many fathers in the Bible, including Abraham, Isaac, and Jacob, also rewarded the faithfulness of their children with a declared blessing and prophetic words about their future.

Children are often watching our actions more than listening to our words. It is amazing how many who disrespect their parents are often disrespected by their children when they become seniors. The saying, "what goes around comes around" is often true. Adults must be careful how they treat their parents as seniors because their treatment of their parents will often come back to haunt them.

The Boomerang

According to Merriam Webster's Dictionary, one of the definitions of a boomerang is, "an act or utterance that backfires on the originator." If you are a senior and you are being mistreated by others, those persons had better get ready for the boomerang because what they are doing to you, will inevitably return to them.

Prayer

Heavenly Father,

I come before You, asking You to pour down a special blessing upon individuals who have been a blessing in my life and in the lives of other seniors. Bless them in their going out and in their coming in. Bless the work of their hands. Shield them with favor on all sides and allow whatever they do to prosper. Let their light break forth as the noonday, their health spring forth speedily whenever they are unwell, and answer them quickly when they call.

In Jesus Christ's name.

Chapter Eight

Arise and Shine: The Glorious Golden Years

*Y*ou made it! You have already gotten through many perils, persecutions, deceptions, and pain. Glory to God! I believe you have something to thank God for and celebrate about. What you survived has left many others broken.

You Are A Survivor

Perhaps you were a part of the baby-boomer generation (1946–1964) and saw the likes of the Vietnam War, The Civil Rights Movement, and the first men to walk on the moon and lived in a time that some may call economic prosperity. Or perhaps you may be a part of the Traditionalist Generation (1900–1945) and had firsthand experience and perhaps even participated in World Wars I and II and experienced the Great Depression and the hardship of rationing. You have seen it all; the good times and bad times. On occasion, it may have been a combination of both, as Charles Dickens mentioned in his novel *A Tale of Two Cities*:

> It was the best of times, it was the worst of times, it was the age of wisdom, it was the age of foolishness, it was the epoch of belief, it was the epoch of incredulity, it was the season of Light, it was the season of Darkness, it was the spring of hope, it was the winter of despair...

In any instance, you experienced both pleasure and pain and you made it through. God is the Alpha and the Omega so what He has begun in you, He is well able to finish.

The Glorious Golden Years

So why would I call the latter years the *glorious golden years*? For many reasons. How does God Himself view you? He speaks of your wisdom in Job 12:12, "With the ancient is wisdom; And in length of days understanding." He sees a unique beauty in your grey hairs, "the beauty of old men is the grey head"

(Prov. 20:29), and He firmly declares that you should receive honor, "Thou shalt rise up before the hoary head, and honour the face of the old man, and fear thy God: I am the Lord" (Lev. 19:32). God also promises to give you dreams, "...your old men shall dream dreams..." (Joel 2:28), and promises to always be with you, "And even to your old age I am he; and even to hoar hairs will I carry you: I have made, and I will bear; even I will carry, and will deliver you" (Isa. 46:4). Who are we to have a different opinion if God Himself sees such splendor in the latter years?

A Time to Arise

After working hard for many years, I see this as a time to rest and spend more time in the presence of the Lord. It is not a time for me to be idle but rather to focus my undivided attention on ensuring that I concentrate on fulfilling God's assignment for my life. The latter years are a glorious time to maximize the spiritual moments and develop an intimacy with God you may have never had before. This glorious time is a time to focus on the things of real importance in life such as the kingdom of God, "But seek ye first the kingdom of God, and His righteousness; and all these things shall be added unto you" (Matt. 6:33), as well as family and friends.

Do not ever convince yourself you are useless when you have so much to offer. Sometimes, it is after many years of *trial and error* that we begin to see what we are gifted with and what God's purpose is for our lives. These glorious golden years may be a time to refocus on and pursue something that we have always wanted to do. This is especially true if you are gifted in many areas. I worked in human resources for many years, but I realized I also had a gift for teaching. Upon retiring, I smoothly transitioned into the role of a teacher because the training I had received and the gift of God had already prepared me for that role. Continually ask God to redeem any time that you have lost.

The glorious golden years is a time to continue to assemble with other believers until you are absolutely unable to do so for, "Those that be planted in the house of the Lord shall flourish in the courts of our God. They shall still bring forth fruit in old age; they shall be fat and flourishing" (Ps. 92:14).

This is also a glorious time to spend imparting your wisdom to your grandchildren and other youths in society for, "Children's children are the crown of old men; and the glory of children are their fathers" (Prov. 17:6). Even if you are in a nursing home, God will still place people around you to whom you can minister the Gospel.

We do not have to expect sickness to come into our lives simply because we are now old. The Scripture states that King David, "...died in a good old age, full of days, riches, and honour: and Solomon his son reigned in his stead" (1 Chron. 29:28). However, in any circumstance we may find ourselves in, we can rest knowing that God is still in control and that *this too shall pass.*

Most importantly, these glorious golden years are for not only enjoyment but also for preparing for the future. Our time on earth is momentary when compared to the time we will spend in eternity.

Jesus states in Mark 8:36–37, "For what shall it profit a man, if he shall gain the whole world, and lose his own soul? Or what shall a man give in exchange for his own soul?" This is not the time to focus attention simply on the things of this world and spend eternity in hell, when the alternative is so easily obtained, "...if thou shalt confess with thy mouth the Lord Jesus, and shalt believe in thine heart that God hath raised him from the dead, thou shalt be saved" (Romans 10:9).

Yes, I am loving my age. And regardless of your age, you should be loving yours too. So arise and shine my fellow seniors. Make the most of each moment and rest assured that the best is yet to come.

Daily To-Do List and Action Plan

1. Read Isaiah 60:1-22.
2. Give God thanks for His blessings and that He will receive glory out of any situation in your life.
3. Maximize the time by spending more time in the presence of God through prayer and meditating on the scriptures.
4. Pursue the things you always wanted to do.
5. Continue to assemble with other believers of Christ.
6. Impart your wisdom to other generations.
7. Trust God and know that even in ill health, you are never alone.

Chapter Nine

Bible Promises for the Aging

We are on Satan's hit list from the day we are born. Just as it would not be wise to go to war with no weaponry, it is unadvisable to go through life without utilizing the weapons that God has given to believers. One such weaponry is the sword of the Spirit which is the Word of God. If we want to defeat the enemy, we must utilize our sword.

Jesus, himself used this weapon in the wilderness against Satan. There is a rhema word in the scriptures for every situation you may be faced with. Ask God to reveal the scripture that is for the situation you are dealing with. Stand on the promises found in those scriptures, do not be distracted or allow the enemy to discourage you. Remain grounded in God's Word.

The following are wonderful scriptures for issues you may be faced with.

Comfort

"Blessed be the God and Father of our Lord Jesus Christ, the Father of mercies and God of all comfort, who comforts us in all our tribulation, that we may be able to comfort those who are in any trouble, with the comfort with which we ourselves are comforted by God" (2 Cor. 1:3-4 NKJV).

Death

"Jesus said unto her, I am the resurrection, and the life: he that believeth in me, though he were dead, yet shall he live" (John 11:25).

"In my Father's house are many mansions: if it were not so, I would have told you. I go to prepare a place for you. And if I go and prepare a place for you, I will come again, and receive you unto myself; that where I am, there ye may be also" (John 14:2–3).

"Marvel not at this: for the hour is coming, in which all that are in the graves shall hear his voice, and shall come forth; they that have done good, unto resurrection of life, and they that have done evil, unto the resurrection of damnation" (John 5:28–29),

"For to me to live is Christ, and to die is gain" (Phil. 1:21).

"Yea, though I walk through the valley of the shadow of death, I will fear no evil: for though art with me, thy rod and thy staff they comfort me" (Ps. 23:4).

Descendants

"The children of thy servants shall continue, and their seed shall be established before thee" (Ps. 102:28).

"And their seed shall be known among the Gentiles, and their offspring among the people: all that see them shall acknowledge them, that they are the seed which the Lord hath blessed" (Isa. 61:9).

"Lift up thine eyes round about, and see: all they gather themselves together, they come to thee: thy sons shall come from far, and thy daughters shall be nursed at thy side" (Isa. 60:4).

"I will pour My Spirit upon thy seed and My blessing upon **thine** offspring: and they shall spring up as among the grass, as willows by the watercourses. One shall say, 'I am the Lord's'; another shall call himself by the name of Jacob; and another shall subscribe with his hand, unto the Lord, and surname himself by the name of Israel" (Isa. 44:3-5).

"And all your children shall be taught of the Lord; and great shall be the peace of thy children" (Isa. 54:13).

"But the mercy of the Lord is from everlasting to everlasting upon them that fear Him, and His righteousness to children's children" (Ps. 103:17).

Fear

"Fear thou not; for I am with thee: be not dismayed; for I am thy God: I will strengthen thee; yea, I will uphold thee with the right hand of my righteousness" (Isa. 41:10).

Forgiveness

"If we confess our sins, He is faithful and just to forgive us our sins and cleanse us from all unrighteousness" (1 John 1:9).

"As far as the east is from the west, so far hath he removed our transgressions from us" (Ps. 103:12).

God's Love

"For God so loved the world that he gave his only begotten Son, that whosoever believeth in him shall not perish, but have everlasting life" (John 3:16).

<u>Healing</u>

"'For I will restore health unto thee, and I will heal thee of thy wounds,' saith the Lord; because they called thee an Outcast, saying, 'This is Zion, whom no man seeketh after'" (Jer. 30:17).

"Bless the Lord, O my soul, And forget not all His benefits: Who forgiveth all thine iniquities, Who healeth all thy diseases" (Ps. 103:2-3).

"Behold, I will bring it health and cure, and I will cure them, and will reveal unto them the abundance of peace and truth" (Jer. 33:6).

"O Lord my God, I cried unto thee, and thou hast healed me" (Ps. 30:2).

"Have mercy upon me, O Lord; for I am weak; O Lord, heal me; for my bones are vexed" (Ps. 6:2).

"He healeth the broken in heart, and bindeth up their wounds" (Ps. 147:3).

"But he was wounded for our transgressions, he was bruised for our iniquities: the chastisement of our peace was upon him; and with his stripes we are healed" (Isa. 53:5).

Honor

"Thou shalt rise up before the hoary head, and honour the face of the old man, and fear thy God: I am the Lord" (Lev. 19:32).

"Hearken unto thy father that begat thee, and despise not thy mother when she is old" (Prov. 23:22).

"Honour thy Father and thy mother: that thy days may be long upon the land which the Lord thy God giveth thee" (Exod. 20:12).

Long Life

"Because he hath set his love upon me...because he had known my name... With long life I will satisfy him and show him my salvation" (Ps. 91:14, 16).

"Thou shalt come to thy grave in a full age, like a shock of corn cometh in his season" (Job 5:26).

"And thou shalt go to thy fathers in peace; thou shalt be buried in a good old age" (Gen. 15:15).

"And Moses was 120 years old when he died: his eyes were not dim, nor his natural force abated." (Deut. 34:7).

"What man is he that desireth life, and loveth many days, that he may see good? Keep thy tongue from evil, and thy lips from speaking guile" (Ps. 34:12–13).

Loneliness

"Fear thou not; for I am with thee, be not dismayed; for I am thy God; I will strengthen thee, yea, I will help thee, yea, I will uphold thee with the right hand of my righteousness" (Isa. 41:10).

"Who shall separate us from the love of Christ? Shall tribulation, or distress, or persecution, famine or nakedness, or peril, or sword?" (Rom. 8:35).

"Nor height, nor depth, nor any creature, shall be able to separate us from the love of God, which is in Christ Jesus our Lord" (Rom. 8:39).

"When my father and my mother forsake me, then the Lord will take me up" (Ps. 27:10).

"I will not leave you comfortless: I will come to you" (John 14:18).

Overcoming Temptation

"Blessed is the man that endureth temptation: for when he is tried, he shall receive the crown of life, which the Lord hath promised to them that love him" (James 1:12).

"There hath no temptation taken you but such as is common to man: but God is faithful, who will not suffer you to be tempted above that ye are able, but will with the temptation also make a way to escape, that ye may be able to bear it" (1 Cor. 10:13).

Peace

"The Lord bless thee, and keep thee: The Lord make his face to shine upon thee, and be gracious unto thee: The Lord lift up his countenance upon thee, and give thee peace" (Num. 6:24–26).

"Peace I leave with you, my peace I give unto you; not as the world giveth, give I unto you.

Let not your heart be troubled, neither let it be afraid" (John 14:27).

"I will both lay me down in peace, and sleep: for thou, Lord, only makest me dwell in safety" (Ps. 4:8).

"Thou wilt keep him in perfect peace, whose mind is stayed on thee: because he trusted in thee" (Isa. 26:3).

Praise and Worship

"Both young men, and maidens; old men, and children: Let them praise the name of the Lord: for his name alone is excellent; his glory is above the earth and heaven" (Ps. 148:12–13).

Protection

"God is our refuge and strength, a very present help in trouble" (Ps. 46:1).

"Thou art my hiding place; thou shalt preserve me from trouble; thou shalt compass me about with songs of deliverance" (Ps. 32:7).

"The Lord shall fight for you, and ye shall hold your peace" (Exod. 14:14).

"So that we may boldly say, The Lord is my helper, and I will not fear what man shall do unto me" (Heb. 13:6).

Salvation of Loved Ones

"For I will contend with him that contendeth with thee, and I will save thy children" (Isa. 49:25).

Strength

"He giveth power to the faint; and to them that have no might he increaseth strength" (Isa. 40:29).

"Who satisfieth thy mouth with good things; so that thy youth is renewed like the eagle's" (Ps. 103:5).

"And now, behold, the Lord hath kept me alive, as he said, these 45 years...and now, lo, I am this day 85 years old. As yet I am as strong this day...as my strength was then, even so is my strength now, for war, both to go out, and to come in" (Josh. 14:10).

"And even to your old age I am he; and even to hoar hairs will I carry you: I have made, and I will bear; even I will carry, and will deliver you" (Isa. 46:4).

Sustenance

"But my God shall supply all your need according to his riches in glory by Christ Jesus" (Phil. 4:19).

"For the Lord God is a sun and shield: The Lord will give grace and glory: No good thing will he withhold from them that walk uprightly" (Ps. 84:11).

"And God is able to make all grace abound toward you; that ye, always having all sufficiency in all things, may abound to every good work" (2 Cor. 9:8).

"The thief cometh not, but for to steal, and to kill, and to destroy: I am come that they might have life, and that they might have it more abundantly" (John 10:10).

"But seek ye first the kingdom of God, and His righteousness; and all these things shall be added unto you" (Matt. 6:33).

"I have been young, and now am old; Yet have I not seen the righteous forsaken, nor his seed begging bread" (Ps. 37:25).

"Now unto him that is able to do exceeding abundantly above all that we ask or think, according to the power that worketh in us..." (Eph. 3:20).

Wisdom and Health for the Mind

"With the ancient is wisdom; and in length of days understanding" (Job 12:12).

"For God hath not given us the spirit of fear; but of power, and of love, and of a sound mind" (2 Tim. 1:7).

"For the weapons of our warfare are not carnal, but mighty through God to the pulling down of strong holds; casting down imaginations, and every high thing that exalteth itself against the knowledge of God, and bringing into captivity every thought to the obedience of Christ..." (2 Cor. 10:4–5).

Chapter Ten

Famous Quotes on Aging

The following are a few famous quotes for you to enjoy.

*"You don't stop laughing when you grow old, you grow old when you stop laughing." – **George Bernard Shaw***

*"Maybe it's true that life begins at fifty. But everything else begins to wear out, fall out and spread out." – **Phyllis Diller***

*"Wisdom is the reward for surviving our own stupidity." – **Brian Rathbone***

*"Wisdom comes with winters." – **Oscar Wilde***

"You know you are getting old when the candles cost more than the cake." – **Bob Hope**

"Growing old is compulsory – growing up is optional." – **Bob Monkhouse**

"Embrace aging." – **Mitch Albom**

"Never tease an old dog: He might have one last bite left." – **Robert A. Heinlein**

"If I'd known I was going to live this long, I'd have taken better care of myself." – **Anonymous**

"An archeologist is the best husband any woman can have; the older she gets, the more interested he is in her." – **Agatha Christie**

"Don't let aging get you down. It's too hard to get back up." – **John Wagner**

"Aging is an issue of mind over matter. If you don't mind, it doesn't matter." – **Mark Twain**

"Old age is always 15 years older than I am." – **Oliver Wendell Holmes**

Chapter Eleven

Poems About Aging

On Aging
By Maya Angelou
(An excerpt of the poem)

When you see me sitting quietly,
Like a sack left on the shelf,
Don't think I need your chattering.
I'm listening to myself.
Hold! Stop! Don't pity me!
Hold! Stop your sympathy!
Understanding if you got it,
Otherwise I'll do without it!
When my bones are stiff and aching,
And my feet won't climb the stair,
I will only ask one favor:
Don't bring me no rocking chair.

All The World's a Stage
By William Shakespeare
(from *As You Like It,* spoken by Jaques)
(An excerpt of the poem)

All the world's a stage,
And all the men and women merely players;
They have their exits and their entrances;
And one man in his time plays many parts,
His acts being seven ages. At first the infant,
Mewling and puking in the nurse's arms;
And then the whining school-boy, with his satchel
And shining morning face, creeping like snail
Unwillingly to school. And then the lover,
Sighing like furnace, with a woeful ballad
Made to his mistress' eyebrow. Then a soldier,
Full of strange oaths, and bearded like the pard,
Jealous in honour, sudden and quick in quarrel,
Seeking the bubble reputation
Even in the cannon's mouth. And then the justice,
In fair round belly with good capon lin'd,
With eyes severe and beard of formal cut,
Full of wise saws and modern instances;
And so he plays his part.

Rabbi Ben Ezra
By Robert Browning
(An excerpt of the poem)

Grow old along with me!
The best is yet to be,
The last of life, for which the first was made:
Our times are in His hand
Who saith "A whole I planned,
Youth shows but half; trust God: see all, nor
be afraid!"

Chapter Twelve

Legacy Statements

My words of wisdom for my future generations are:

<u>Spiritual</u>

_____

_____

_____

_____

_____

_____

_____

_____

Finances

_____

_____

_____

_____

_____

_____

_____

_____

_____

Career

_____

_____

_____

_____

_____

_____

_____

_____

_____

_____

Health

_____

_____

_____

_____

_____

_____

_____

_____

_____

Overall

_____

_____

_____

_____

_____

_____

_____

_____

_____

Chapter Thirteen

Family Tree

References

Dr. Leroy Thompson Sr., *How To Speak The Word Of God With The Voice Of Jesus* (Ever Increasing Word Ministries, Darrow, Louisiana, 1998)

"Glass ceiling." "Merriam-Webster.com" accessed July 13, 2019, https://www.merriam-webster.com/dictionary/glass%20ceiling.

"Baker's Evangelical Dictionary of Biblical Theology – Bible Dictionary." "StudyLight.org" accessed June 15, 2019, https://www.studylight.org/dictionaries/bed.html?s=Yases.

"Boomerang." Merriam-Webster.com, accessed March 20, 2020, https://www.merriam-webster.com/dictionary/boomerang.

Karina Martinez-Carter, "How the Elderly are Treated Around the World," The Week, July 23, 2013, http://theweek.com/articles/462230/how-elderly-are-treated-around-world.

"Timex Corp." AdAge Encyclopedia, September 15, 2003, https://adage.com/article/adage-encyclopedia/timex-corp/98905.

Gregg Laurie, "Remorse or Repentance?" The Christian Post, January 4, 2012, https:www.christianpost.com/news/remorse-or-repentance.html.

"Culturally Appropriate Geriatric Care Assessment," Stanford School of Medicine Ethnogeriatrics 2020, accessed September 20, 2019, https://geriatrics.stanford.edu/ethnomed/korean/assessment.html.

"Proposed working definition of an older person in Africa for the MDS Project," World Health Organization, accessed August 15, 2019, https://www.who.int/healthinfo/survey/ageingdefnolder/en/.

W. Andrew Achenbaum, "A History of Ageism Since 1969," Generations, Fall 2015"

Browning, Robert, "Rabbi Ben Ezra," ed. William Adams Slade (New York, T. Y. Crowell & Company, 1902).

"Aging Quotes," Good Reads, accessed August 20, 2019, https://www.goodreads.com/quotes/tag/aging.

R. W. Shamback. "You Don't Have Any Troubles, All You Need Is Faith In God," Dominion Camp Meeting, July 7, 1992, https://youtube/rz76qqwihwc.

Scriven, Joseph M., "What a Friend we have in Jesus," *Sing to The Lord*, Lillenas Publishing Company, 1973.

Duffield, Jr., George, "Stand Up, Stand Up for Jesus," *Sing to The Lord*, Lillenas Publishing Company, 1973.

Jessica Lindsay, "What generation am I and what do they mean? From Baby Boomers to Millennials," METRO Lifestyle, January 29, 2018, http://metro.co.uk/2018/01/29/generation-mean-baby-boomers-millenials-726464/.

"Zogen." "Strong's Concordance" https://biblehub.com/hebrew/2207.htm.

References

"Geras." "Strong's Concordance" https://biblehub.com/greek/1094.htm.

"TETELESTAI – IT IS FINISHED! PAID IN FULL!" Preceptaustin, April 5, 2013, https://preceptaustin.wordpress.com/2013/04/05/tetelestai-it-is-finished-paid-in-full/.

Ann Spangler, "El Roi Is the God Who Sees Me," Faithgateway, February 24, 2017, https://www.faithgateway.com/el-roi-god-who-sees-me/#.xte-ix4pawa.

Mayo Angelou, "On Aging," in *The Complete Collected Poems of Maya Angelou* (New York: Random House, 1994).

Robert H. Schuller, *Turning Hurts Into Halos and Scars Into Stars* (Thomas Nelson, Inc., Nashville, Tennessee, 1999)

Robert A. Schuller, *Getting Through What You're Going Through* (Thomas Nelson, Inc. Nashville, Tennessee, 1986)

Jose Luis Navajo, *Mondays With My Old Pastor* (Thomas Nelson, Inc. Nashville, Tennessee, 2012)

Dr. Charles Stanley, *Walking With God* (Thomas Nelson, Inc., Nashville, Tennessee, 2012)

Chris Hodges, *Fresh Air* (Tyndale Momentum, Tulsa, Oklahoma, 2012)

John Dickson, *Humilitas* (Zondervan, Grand Rapids, Michigan, 2011)

Richard Rohr, *The Universal Christ* (Convergent Books, New York, New York, 2019)

R.T. Kendall, *Controlling The Tongue* (Charisma House, Lake Mary, Florida, 2007)

Dr. Mike Brown, *Avoiding The Snare* (Diamond Publishing, Mobil, Alabama, 2007)

Andrew Wommack, *How To Find, Follow, Fulfill God's Will* (Harrison House Publishers, Tulsa, Oklahoma, 2013)

Lee Strobel, *The Case For Miracles* (Zondervan, Grand Rapids, Michigan, 2018)

Tripp Bowden, *Freddie and Me* (Skyhorse Publishing, New York, New York, 2009)

Michael Ricker, *A Heart A Flame* (Johnson Printing Company, Brandenton, Florida, 2004)

Bob Farr, *Renovate Or Die* (Abingdon Press, Nashville, Tennessee, 2011)

Diane Muldrow, *Everything I Need To Know I Learned From A Little Golden Book* (Golden Books, New York, New York, 2013)

Dan Tanner, *A Collection Of Quotes Compiled by Dan Tanner* (Unpublished, Blashear, Georgia, 1999)

Al Holley, "Come Next Spring" (Twelve Oaks Studios, Marietta, Georgia, 1980, Vinyl LP Album)

Al Holley, "Friends Like You" (Twelve Oaks Studios, Marietta, Georgia, 1980, Vinyl LP Album)

About the Author

A ndrea Clarke Pratt retired in 2018 after more than 30 years in the corporate world. She then pursued the field of Education and is currently teaching at a local High School.

Andrea knew in her early teens God had a plan for her life. Although she strayed for some years, she rededicated her life to Jesus Christ in her late 20's and began to grow in the knowledge of His love. Her hunger for the Word of God led her to complete a Master's Degree in Theology.

Andrea is the daughter of Reverend Yvonne Clarke and deceased father, Deacon Kingsley Clarke. Andrea and her husband, Pastor Edward Pratt, reside on the beautiful island of New Providence in The Bahamas and are the parents of 4 children. Her favorite scripture is Isaiah 41:10 "Fear thou not; for I am with thee; be not dismayed; for I am thy God; I will strengthen thee; yea I will help thee, yea, I will uphold thee with the right hand of my righteousness."

Contact:
P. O. Box N-8579
Colony Village
Nassau, New Providence
The Bahamas

adpratt6@gmail.com

CPSIA information can be obtained
at www.ICGtesting.com
Printed in the USA
LVHW082044031120
670476LV00004BA/272